Praise for Extinction

Geza Tatrallyay's third collection, *Extinction*, has the feeling of prophecy. Brave and unflinching, these poems catapult into our reluctant consciousness, making inevitable a series of bold questions about the world our grandchildren will inherit. Interspersed are poems of love and gratefulness, a stunning contrast that even further calls the reader to action. These poems do not hide behind the decorative or the oblique. Composed with considerable poetic skill, they meet us head on.

Ina Anderson, author of Journey Into Space

Geza experiments with language as a painter explores color and his poetry reflects his broad experience in diverse cultures.

Rebecca McMeekin, PoemTown Randolph Organizer

EXTINCTION

EXTINCTION

Poems

by
Geza Tatrallyay

Foreword by Peter Fox Smith

Copyright © 2019 P.R.A. Publishing

All Rights Reserved.

No part of this book may be reproduced or transmitted by any means, electronic or mechanical, including photocopying, recording or by any information storage and retrieval system, without express permission from the publisher.

ISBN: 978-1941416-19-8 (Electronic Book)
ISBN: 978-1941416-18-1 (Print)
Library of Congress Catalog Number: 2019931786

P.R.A. Publishing
P.O. Box 211701
Martinez, GA 30917
www.prapublishing.com

Cover photo by Kevin Walsh – Oxford, England.
Cover design by Laura MacDonald.
Interior design by Medlar Publishing Solutions Pvt Ltd., India.

The following poems have been previously published: "Haiku: Milky Way," *Bywords*, October 2017; "The Trout," *Polar Expressions*, December 2017; "Saturn," *Poem Town Randolph Anthology*, April 2018; "The Witching Hour," *Existere Journal* 37.2 Spring/Summer 2018.
"The world is a dangerous place"; "Haiku: Raqqa"; "There is no second chance"; "Extinction"; "Drowning"; "The Dragonfly"; "Haiku: Statement of Godlessness"; "Haiku: Piss"; and "Unhinged Leaders" *Grey Borders Magazine*, August 2018.

Printed in the United States.

For Sophia

Acknowledgements

I am deeply grateful to Lucinda Clark for her continued support for my poetry, and her willingness to now publish this, the third of my collections. Lucinda and her team at P.R.A. Publishing have turned all three of my poetic volumes, starting with Cello's Tears in 2015, Sighs and Murmurs in 2018 and now Extinction, into beautiful, very readable books. A special thanks goes to Laura MacDonald who did much of the work to bring *Extinction* into publishing shape and to Sundar Maruthu for the fine editing and layout.

And my sincerest thanks goes to my friend, Peter Fox Smith, for the insightful Foreword he wrote for my book. Peter is, in my humble opinion, one of the best living poets in the USA today, even though he is known more for his work with one of my other passions, opera. Also, to Ina Anderson and Rebecca McMeekin for their positive comments about my work.

Table of Contents

Foreword . . . . *xiii*

Part I. The World

Witching Hour 3
Haiku: Calving Glaciers 4
Haiku: End of Day 5
Haiku: Milky Way 6
Sky 7
Haiku: Total Eclipse 8
Let The Day Begin! 9
Haiku: Polar Ice Cap 10
Saturn 11
Haiku: Fog Sits On The Bay 12
Storm 13
Storm II 14
Haiku: Above the Clouds 15
Pristine Snowflakes… 16
Haiku: Frosty Night 17
Haiku: Eons Ago 18
Melting Polar Ice Cap 19

Table of Contents

Haiku: Crystalline Snowflakes 21
Threatening Pond 22
Haiku: Tsunami Warning 23
Paradise, California 24
Haiku: April Morning's Snow 26
Thunder and Lightning 27
Haiku: When Will Mankind Learn? 28

Part II. Species

Extinction 31
Mosquito 32
The Trout 33
The Dragonfly 34
Reluctant Weeder 35
The Ultimate Invasive Species 37
Stamp Collecting 38
Haiku: An Army of Ants 40
The World is a Dangerous Place... 41
Haiku: piss 43
Unhinged Leaders 44
Haiku: Raqqa 45
Sarin in Syria 46
Elusive Anthropoid... 48
Humans and Rats 50
Crayfish in the Pond 51
Haiku: Hunting Season 53
A Cockroach Winked At Me... 54
Venice, Under Siege 55
Hitchhiking in the Galaxy... 56
Haiku: Cretacean Fantasy 57

Table of Contents

Part III. Personal

Fallen Leaves 61
Haiku: Statement of Godlessness 62
Haiku: Billowing Sail 63
Forty Years 64
Requiem 66
Nihil 67
Haiku: Like the Sun 68
The Torment of Time 69
Haiku: Unhung Noose 70
Drowning 71
Falling 72
Haiku: Pelting Rain 73
After The Lights Are Out… 74
Haiku: Creepy, Ghoulish Thoughts 75
Time Shuffles Us… 76
Haiku: Garlic Love 77
Like Romeo… 78
A Cacophony of Aches and Assorted Ills… 79
Haiku: Wind-Blown Grains of Grit 80
Boring Time 81
Haiku: Old Age 82
A Sharp Seashell… 83
The Four Seasons 84
Beauty 85
The Fire 87
When I Die 88
Haiku: Dawn's Foggy *Frisson* *90*
There Is No Second Chance… 91

About the Author 92
About Peter Fox Smith 93

Foreword

Nearly fifty years ago Geza Tatrallyay and I could have passed each other unwittingly in Harvard Yard but we did not meet until reading at a poetry recitation in Vermont last year. Immediately, I recognized similarities in our concerns pertaining to the perilous, irresponsible human condition, the fate of our planet, and for everything that lives upon it.

The carefully selected cover of Geza's third volume of poetry, *Extinction*, and the author's cogent introduction reveals its tripart contents: destroying our earth, extinction of all life, and, finally, poignant reflections on his own mortality. The wonder of this book, however, transcends the obvious gloom with the inclusion of poems detailing the incomparable beauty of our universe and the power of love to make human life a meaningful experience.

The "Witching Hour", the book's first poem, impresses me for two significant reasons. The major theme is stated without a single excessive word in three compact stanzas: "Is this the witching hour, the turning point," in "…destroying our one earth". Also, what a pleasure to read a poem with a strict form and fitting meter. The form of his poems is important to Tatrallyay and is only one reason why he is

Foreword

so inclined to haiku, which requires saying much in a few words. In three lines and seventeen syllables as follows:

> *We keep polluting:*
> *storms, floods and fires blight our earth –*
> *when will mankind learn?*

Numerous dark images dominate this first part, "evening shadows," "black hole," "terrible night," yet the poet reminds us of the beauty of the universe with such a line as "the royal sun's brilliant arrival." So why do we not cease our selfish lifestyle?

Part Two opens with the title poem, again admirably strict in blank verse with a telling alliteration of the letter "r" in the third line of the tercet:

> *I can picture the mighty mastodon,*
> *the towering, ivoried, hairy beast*
> *that ruled and roamed this primal earth*

After a four-stanza declaration of "Extinction", in the following poem, "Mosquito", Geza shares a light-hearted moment by killing a mosquito which has bitten him but whose relatives spend the remainder of the summer exacting their revenge. Geza Tatrallyay loves the greatest music, as do I, and Schubert, Mozart, Verdi, and Bach have their place in his poems and what an unforgettable image is his *Cello's Tears*, the title of Geza's first collection of poems. In this second part a favorite of mine is "Reluctant Weeder". Shamed by his wife into weeding, Geza lists twenty-eight exotically named weeds, which in true Darwinian words ultimately will dominate as the survival of the fittest. Nevertheless, Part Two leaves no doubt that humans have made their one world into a very dangerous place.

Foreword

Geza Tatrallyay contemplates his own demise in the third, final part making it clear in several poems that the love he and his wife, Marcia, share is what gives purpose and meaning to a human life which will end. His poem "Requiem" is a taut, ten lines of three syllables each except for line ten which is an imposing, conclusive question mark. This powerful, little poem is for me a condensation of human ultimate concern. "When I die /will I hear/the Mozart/Requiem/or Verdi's/Or simply/will it be/the silence/of nothing/?"

Geza's poems do confront our human ultimate concerns of Mother Earth, life, love, death, and the meaning of existence. There are the doomsday poems, an unmistakable wake-up call, if not already too late, and poems on the beauty of our cosmos along with the fleeting joys of love open to being husband, father, and grandfather. This book makes it clear where Geza is coming from, where he is going, why, and his wonderful, compact poems demonstrate what poetry is and ought to be. What a pleasure to have found a like-minded friend making his way down the same road.

Peter Fox Smith
North Pomfret, Vermont
January 2019

Part I
The World

Witching Hour

Is this the witching hour, the turning point,
when the simmering seas boil, spill across
the cauldron's brim to flood this verdant earth:
corpses of frogs and fish, seals and birds,
our detritus, plastics and rotting hulls
wash up with the silt to bury my feet.

Is this the witching hour, the turning point,
when wildfires spread, raging across the land
and consume forests and fields, roads and towns,
killing with burning heat and acrid smoke
all life they find in homes or barns or nests
or frantically fleeing the fated end.

Is this the witching hour, the turning point:
we know damn well it is, but do nothing—
we continue our hedonistic lives,
complicit in destroying our one earth.

Haiku: Calving Glaciers

glaciers calve, like cows:
but these children, too, all die,
like we, who strew filth

Haiku: End of Day

evening shadows play:
the splendor of the sunset,
the chill of the night

Haiku: Milky Way

A starry scar stares
back at me from the black hole
of the endless sky

Sky

Apple blossoms beckon,
near me, on dark fingers,

as twilight floods the world:

with the lingering light,
the blue-grey silhouettes,
the mountains behind, lift
a polychromic sky—

rose and pink and orange,
mauve fading to lilac,
lavender to indigo…

But twilight always rules:

the color symphony
is slowly drowned out, first,
by the frogs' crescendo,
then the terrible night.

Haiku: Total Eclipse

the moon shrouds the sun
bringing darkness to the world
an omen: for what?

Let The Day Begin!

Dawn seeps slowly over distant mountains

but in the long night's lingering stillness,
leaves dare not rustle, nor birds start their song,
as all nature awaits the royal sun's
brilliant arrival, the world's conquest.

We are ready now: let the day begin!

Haiku: Polar Ice Cap

the polar ice cap
is thawing into the sea
turn on the AC

Saturn

(hommage à Cassini)

we on earth know you better now,
friend Saturn, thanks to Cassini,
the prolific astronomer,
the speck of a spacecraft that flew
in solitude to visit you
through the silent universe…

you, god, so apt for modern times,
with your eclectic collection
of more than sixty stunning moons,
and that colorful alphabet
of rings of icy particles,
yet so distant, so out of reach…

could you be the only planet
that rears life in our neighborhood
or perhaps the whole universe?
your moons, Enceladus, Titan,
have given us the happy hope
that we are not alone out there.

Haiku: Fog Sits On The Bay

fog sits on the bay
the starting day is opaque
and lugubrious

Storm

menacing lightning
zigzags across the sky

thundering hooves of hell
trample this beaten earth

torrential rain washes
our human filth away

Storm II

a wild storm rages
in the humid night
I wake to a world renewed

Haiku: Above the Clouds

the far away world
loses its meaning
when I climb above the clouds

Pristine Snowflakes...

Pristine snowflakes float from a gray sky,
blanketing the world in nuptial white:

bedecked in my Sorels, I step outside
and violate this virginal landscape
crushing crystals, churning up dirt and stones,
turning the frozen natural order
of the microcosm where my boots alight
into liquefying, heaving anarchy

the big question, as my boots crunch along:
will the next snowfall restore this beauty?

Haiku: Frosty Night

the night is frosty
I wake to snow on the ground
spring is far away

Haiku: Eons Ago

eons ago we played
now we only weep
for the planet we destroyed

Melting Polar Ice Cap

In the pristine air of Greenland
the squeaky crunch of my footsteps
on the glacier's crisp surface ice
ends with the sloshing of wet slush

While in more inhabited lands
the soft footfall of city shoes
on concrete sidewalks, or walkways,
metamorphoses overnight
to mad splashing as floodwaters
invade parks, streets and foundations
destroying communal living
not just here but everywhere

But the science is clear, my friend:
ice melts when heat accumulates
and is ensnared by CO_2

Mankind just spews out this foul gas
by still burning fossil fuels,
unmindful of consequences

Melting Polar Ice Cap

The irony: our refusal
to change our depraved way of life
will force us to change how we live
as we all scramble to survive
this utter vile devastation
we managed to bring on ourselves

Haiku: Crystalline Snowflakes

In the chilly hush
crystalline snowflakes descend
and die on landing

Threatening Pond

by the light of the smiling moon,
the gemstones in the sky, I see
the black ink spilled across the lawn,

hear crickets chirping, toads croaking,
and a far away loon crooning,
distracting me with their music

the black hole of the pond beckons,
threatens with ominous darkness,
I turn back inside, to the light.

Haiku: Tsunami Warning

tsunami warning:
the wave will wash all away—
let's evacuate

Paradise, California

Paradise, California:
hell fires rage out of control—

the wind whips flames from tree to tree
from bush to bush, from house to house
spreading the scorching inferno
its poisonous smoke, far and wide

the fire consumes all in its path
homes, towns, turn to ash and rubble
trucks and cars melt into liquid
humans and animals dissolve
in fractions of nanoseconds
into oxygen and carbon
some hydrogen and nitrogen
and a few other elements…

toxic fumes float over countries
making mere breathing difficult
contaminating and killing
the living things they penetrate

Paradise, California

many hundreds burn to charcoal
their screams echoing through the night
for weeks thousands remain missing
then the numbers of dead go up
and keep ratcheting up and up

the searing grief of survivors
bursts in a crescendo of tears

the hellish horror of it all

Haiku: April Morning's Snow

April morning's snow
glistens in the joyful sun—
melts by cloudy noon

Thunder and Lightning

When we heard the far-off thunder,
we children used to say, the gods
are bowling on Mount Olympus.

When lightning lit the entire sky,
we would scurry inside and hide:
Jupiter had just bowled a strike.

When torrential rain lashed the earth,
though petrified, we knew deep down
the celestial pantheon wept
for the folly of humankind.

Haiku: When Will Mankind Learn?

We keep polluting:
storms, floods and fires blight our earth—
when will mankind learn?

Part II
Species

Extinction

I can picture the mighty mastodon,
the towering, ivoried, hairy beast
that ruled and roamed this primeval earth

the fierce dinosaurs of the Jurassic,
those huge cold-blooded reptilian beasts
battling each other for primacy

through the microscope of my failing mind
in the imagined black hole of creation
I see tiny single-celled organisms,
the chemical precursors to all life

I ask: when humankind is no longer,
who or what will conceive this strange being
that destroyed earth and all life including
itself as if it had been preordained

Mosquito

A wanton mosquito landed
on the bare skin of my forearm,
attacked my feeling flesh with glee,

in a drunken stupor it gorged
through its proboscis on my blood

I swatted the little bugger
with lightning fury and hate,
and squashed it to oblivion,

unmindful of the perfection
of a timeless, evolved being

Over the long torrid summer
my mosquito's countless mates wreak
their revenge on humanity

The Trout

A lone trout inhabits our pond,
curious about the crayfish,
the rotting leaves by the stone steps.

I approach: a flick of the tail
and it plunges effortlessly
into the unfathomable
depths of the watery black hole.

Back in the house, as I listen
to Franz Schubert's sublime quintet,
I wonder: did the fish arrive
by divine magic, as some believe,
the wave of a wand, a god's hand,
the virgin birth of creation,

or drop, a stray fertilized egg
from the palmate of a mallard,
the sheer necessity of chance,
the mere chance of necessity.

The next year my trout is not there.

The Dragonfly

I found a dragonfly lazing on our screen door:
a Great Blue Skimmer spreading its filigree wings,
flaunting its dazzling long lapis abdomen
soaking up the warming rays of the noonday sun
oblivious to its Jurassic ancestry

I wonder: will my friend's descendants still be here
one hundred and fifty million years from now,
as we disrupt the equilibrium of earth,
insect outliving cocky Homo sapiens,
the destructive devil of the Anthropocene

Reluctant Weeder

I was out in the sun
pulling up weeds today,
shamed to it by my wife

invasives and natives
all must go, be dug out

wild chervil and knapweed,
purple loosestrife, pokeweed,
garlic mustard, burdock,
false indigo, goutweed,
and the giant hogweed,
Louise's swallow-wart,
corn speedwell and fleabane,
crabgrass and curly dock,
bull thistle and cheatgrass,
thistle and burning bush,
jimsonweed and henbit,
purslane and purple cudweed,
stinkgrass and spotted spurge
witchgrass, yellow foxtail,
hairy galinsoga,
and the tree of heaven.

Reluctant Weeder

They are all stunning plants,
many have such grand names,
why banish them, I ask?

Are we not just fighting
relentless, remorseless,
ruthless evolution?

Will this purging of weeds
from our fields, our gardens,
make any difference
in nature's progress?

The fittest will survive
despite all our efforts
to nurture the others.

The Ultimate Invasive Species

weeds and pests proliferate all around,
unmindful of the pretended order
we, the ultimate invasive species,
struggle to impose on our universe:
nature will always win out in the end

Stamp Collecting

I used to collect stamps when I was young,
sit mesmerized on my grandpa's lap,
as he flipped through the crinkling cellophane
separating the pages of albums
carefully tended since he was a boy—

little rectangles, squares, some triangles,
most with sides half perforated, like teeth,
beautifully arranged by country, by set,
lowest denomination first, highest last—

some from countries that no longer exist
or have changed their names, gained independence,
some conquered, some new, split off from others:
Yugoslavia and Tanganyika,
Sikkim and Moldova, Burma, Aden—
strange languages, exotic currencies:
bahts, dongs, forints, meticals and ringgits;

Stamp Collecting

those colors and shapes, pictures of mountains
of flowers, bridges, penguins and leopards,
the ones depicting sports – my favorites,
portraits of kings, queens, famous citizens,
many long departed from earthly life—

some stamps surviving harsh separation
from the missive by soaking in water,
then careful tugging at the four corners,
others tearing, their value diminished,
still others in near perfect condition,
a collector's joy, though franked and now glue-less,

some, pristine, unused, bearing no postmark,
waiting to serve the intended purpose
to take a letter, package or postcard
to a business, a friend, or a love,
or hide forever, the prized possession
of an avid collector, yours truly—

the flow of history, the sciences,
and political geography taught
so ably by little bits of paper;

this habit though, is also now passé
my grandson prefers to watch videos
or play games, send emails on his laptop

a hobby threatened like the polar bear
on that rare pale blue issue from Greenland

Haiku: An Army of Ants

An army of ants
cleans my counter top of crumbs.
Why would I crush them?

The World is a Dangerous Place...

the world is a dangerous place:
hurricanes rage along the coast,
screaming winds topple tall buildings,
tidal waves surge, flooding cities,

the world is a dangerous place:
wildfires burn, drought parches the land,
thirsty flora and fauna die,
bacteria mutate and spread,

the world is a dangerous place:
ships collide, planes fall from the sky,
ICBMs fly overhead,
cyber attacks hack power plants,

the world is a dangerous place:
chemicals mar Kurdish children,
migrants drown escaping terror,
suicide bombers blow up malls,

The World is a Dangerous Place...

the world is a dangerous place:
three hundred and ten million
guns in private hands out to kill
children in schools, folk in churches,
or out shopping or in the park

the world is a dangerous place:
we continue to rape the earth
burn its dirty fossil fuels
sullying its life-giving air,
filling the oceans with plastic

Man is the threat, the destroyer:
is this not pure insanity?

Haiku: Piss

we piss on the world
but it is we who will drink
the piss of the world

Unhinged Leaders

unhinged leaders threaten
with fingers poised to press
the nuclear bomb's button
and devastate the world

Haiku: Raqqa

Raqqa is rubble
bombs and babies scream
the stench of death burns my nose

Sarin in Syria

The chuff-chuff of the chopper gets louder:
panic-stricken, I peek out from my hole
under the rubble of prior attacks,
vainly willing it to disintegrate…

But no, I scream involuntarily:
one of Bashar's dreaded barrel-like bombs
drops from the belly of the flying beast
tugged by gravity toward the shelter
where Douma's vulnerable take cover—
women and children, the old and wounded…

And then I know: I feel it, I smell it:
the acrid burning with every breath,
the bleach-like pungency of chlorine gas—
or is it the fire of sarin, or both?

I look for a cloth to filter the air,
as I hear the helicopter recede
I rush toward the demolished refuge
desperate to unearth my child, my wife,
still breathing, still whole of limb, still alive.

Sarin in Syria

My eyes and lungs burn, my stomach empties,
but I dig deeper with bleeding fingers,
shove broken bricks, piles of plaster aside:
I touch the limp forearm of a woman
and burrow for the fingers that tell all—

I cry and convulse as the horror dawns
and search among the dead for my one son,
finally find him foaming and drooling
in a makeshift hospital—but alive!

They say maybe chlorine mixed with sarin,
chemicals long banned even from battle,
but used here by Assad against his own—
cheered on by Putin, Stalin's successor,

the lily-livered West's supposed red line—
but again there is no retribution
not even a Nuremberg-like trial
to punish this odious genocide.

Elusive Anthropoid...

Even though we destroy
your luscious habitat,

>brother orangutan,
>wise man of the jungle,
>elusive anthropoid,

you gaze at me with peace
and woe and wonder,
sitting there regally
up on your tree-top perch
in the nest you crafted
so skillfully last night—

your flaming orange hair
glistens in the sunlight
before you disappear
in the high canopy
of greens and browns and blues…

Elusive Anthropoid...

how many more sightings,

>brother orangutan,
>wise man of the jungle,
>elusive anthropoid,

before you are extinct,
and then how much longer
until mankind follows?

Humans and Rats

I watch humans
scurrying by
like rats rushing
to a fated
meaningless end

Crayfish in the Pond

Crayfish have invaded our pond:
those ugly arthropods laid siege
and conquered the massive stone steps
painstakingly laid by the Wards
to ease our way to the water

those yabbies now guard the ramparts
big ones like lobsters, little ones—
more than thirty scamper about
on the underwater platform
copulating to multiply
locking claws in brutal battle

when I hesitatingly step
in the water below the falls
the braver ones tickle my toes
testing the intruding giant

Crayfish in the Pond

my grandson watches in horror
but I tell him with a chuckle
these little crawdads are harmless
they have survived on mother earth
for fifty plus million years
since the earliest Eocene

without doubt they will outlive us
and the destruction we have brought
on our planet's environment—
climate change, the melting glaciers,
all the wildfires, tempests and floods

they will just go and hibernate,
hide under the rock in the tarn
to reemerge when the sun smiles
on our wasted world once again

Haiku: Hunting Season

careful in the woods
hunting season is open
for deer, not humans

A Cockroach Winked At Me...

A cockroach winked at me from the closet corner,
brazenly taunting the prejudiced human me:

As the beast darted under the soiled laundry pile,
wild with frenzy, I lifted high a much-scuffed shoe
wanting to crush that pestilent cocky creature—

I threw aside the mountain of grubby garments,
and, like Khrushchev banging his desk at the UN,
in the twilight depths of my disordered wardrobe,
blindly bashed away at visions of the beetle

But the insect escaped, scuttling under the boards,
crusty carapace and gangly legs still intact,
to sneak back and goad my ire yet another day

Venice, Under Siege

Oh, Serenissima, what have we done?

You, City of Water, are under siege:

Seven-storied tour boats crowd your canals,
puking city-loads of eager tourists
doing Europe in ten-day package tours
leaving their detritus for you to drink

We spew gases into the atmosphere
that melt glaciers and cause the seas to rise,
flooding canals, *calli* and piazzas,
eroding the footings of your palazzos

Most serene Queen of the Adriatic,
is your poignant crumbling a harbinger
of our relentless march to extinction?

Hitchhiking in the Galaxy...

(with a deep bow to Douglas Adams)

One trillion plus pounds of conscient human flesh
have hitched a ride on this rock in the Milky Way
hurtling through a dark and dangerous universe:

With uncaring greed, in the human pleasure quest,
this palpitating mass ditches its detritus
polluting the globe's precious land, water and air
necessary for survival of life on earth

Mankind will not need that guide to hitchhiking in the galaxy:
for we are the unwitting architects of our own destruction

Haiku: Cretacean Fantasy

Glide across the sky
glibly, grasping the crest of
a pterodactyl

Part III
Personal

Fallen Leaves

fallen leaves tango in the street
with whirling dust that tears the eyes,

rustle with the strains of the wind,
announcing the advent of fall

and I shiver as I follow
in their wake toward the winter
from which there is no more waking

Haiku: Statement of Godlessness

the devil may come
and take my impious soul
I do not believe

Haiku: Billowing Sail

the billowing sail
speeds my craft through the water
soon our lips will touch

Forty Years

Forty years ago I saw you
across a crowded room
of merry partyers

Your poise and beauty
stood out as to this day—
I loved you then as now

We have traveled the world,
you and I, holding hands,
nested in happy homes,
begat loving children
who are begetting theirs

And still the passion thrills
as those frenzied first nights
of unfettered delight

Forty Years

Your eyes still speak to me
with love each day and night,
I touch your silken skin
and tremble in response,
your thighs envelope me
as your breath titillates
and I melt one more time
inside your loving womb

Only death could smother
you or me, and our love.

Requiem

When I die
will I hear
the Mozart
Requiem
or Verdi's

Or simply
will it be
the silence
of nothing?

NIHIL

Days shorten as time races to the line,
the eternal nihil of the beyond:

Do not weep when I am no longer here,
returned to the mass grave of mother earth,
remember only my lips grazing yours,
our entwined, feeling bodies giving warmth,
the nomadic life of love we lived *à deux*—

a few memories might reside in you
and vaguely linger only while you live
as these poems of love I wrote for you,
before death eagerly shreds them too.

And I, the creator, am nothing again.

Haiku: Like the Sun

each day, like the sun,
you brighten my world:
do not go into the night

The Torment of Time

that dazzling orange orb falls from the sky
mountain silhouettes sketch a horizon
and the world shivers with the chill of night

in the tiptoeing terror of twilight
my frantic fingertips cannot find you
you faded into the nocturnal void

I am left alone with run away thoughts
to face the eternal torment of time

Haiku: Unhung Noose

The innocent smile
of my curious grandson
keeps my noose unhung

Drowning

my submarine screams slosh
inside this aching skull
distant, lugubrious

the water of life bloats
the lungs to near bursting,
the last bubbles reach up
toward a bobbing sun

and the thrashing flesh sinks
into the sediment,
the pain of consciousness
ebbs away to nothing

I exist no longer

Falling

I stand on the edge of the precipice,
look down the rocky face into the void:
far below, the verdant valley calling

Like a long jumper I propel myself
outward into thin air, flailing, kicking,
then I plummet, the body accelerates,
tugged toward extinction by gravity

I gasp for breath as existence speeds by,
an entire lifetime of blistering pain
concentrated in the flash of impact
as consciousness is smashed to smithereens
and I am no longer of the living

Haiku: Pelting Rain

rain pelts on the pane
pulls me from a dream
the opaque terror of night

After The Lights Are Out...

After the lights are out
when I lie still and stiff
and my eyes glaze over
vultures flop down with glee
to peck at rotting flesh
hungry ants and maggots
mop up the stinking mess
till I am dust again

Haiku: Creepy, Ghoulish Thoughts

creepy, ghoulish thoughts
well up in the brain at night:
when will death take me?

Time Shuffles Us...

time shuffles us toward old age:
decrepitude deflates our dreams,
arthritis deforms joints with pain,
skin sags, wrinkles weather the face,
the brain spins its own universe—
your voice seems muffled, far away
but your touch still inflames desire
and our love staves off our demise
from day to day, eternally

Haiku: Garlic Love

my wife says I use
too much garlic in my sauce
I peel one more clove.

Like Romeo...

Like Romeo, I yearn to cling to you,
my Juliet, lust for your silken touch,
your sensual kisses, your soft voice—
I cherish this love that defies the void,
the shrieking black hole of our loneliness,
in this empty, temporal universe,
the existence-devouring solitude
imposed by those perverse, purported gods,
the false idols that dare to cheat our hopes:
the one solace, our chase after that look,
the caress, the shared pleasures that affirm
that for this moment on this spinning globe
at least we are alive and not alone

A Cacophony of Aches and Assorted Ills...

A cacophony of aches and assorted ills
burrows, like worms, or mice, through a rotting body,
disturbing sleep, derailing thought, distorting time

despite it all we go on loving and living
till the weakened organism can cope no longer
and consciousness comes to its sad, preordained end

Haiku: Wind-Blown Grains of Grit

wind-blown grains of grit
tear the eye, sandblast the skin—
like when you left me

Boring Time

the clock has struck midnight
I still sit at my desk
staring at the pistol
I loaded hours ago

will I pull the trigger
or will I chicken out
is the daunting question

boring time marches past
dawn beckons from outside—
bursting inside I scream:
I cannot tolerate
another searing day!

I pick up the pistol
put it to my temple
and…

Haiku: Old Age

skin wrinkles, joints ache,
peeing becomes difficult—
the mind slows, forgets

A Sharp Seashell…

a sharp seashell slashes my sole
my blood oozes into the sand

the next wave washes all away
with infinitesimal dilution

like when my consciousness merges
into the infinite nothing

The Four Seasons

(in Haiku style)

Spring
with spring's ecstasy
I inhale cherry blossoms
when I kiss your skin

Summer
the warmth of the sun
radiates from your body
when I embrace you

Autumn
autumnal colors
augment the day's brilliance—
like you, at my side

Winter
of a wintry night
I long for your silken touch—
but you are not there

Beauty

The morning mist frosting the fen
the sunset glow crowning the hills

the waking song of the wood thrush
the moan of the loon by the moon

the pink peony in your garden
the rusted leaves of the fall forest

a monarch fluttering its wings
a deer dashing across the yard

the air after a spring shower
the waft of my freshly baked bread

the taste of a just picked cherry
or a sip of Chateau Petrus

the six sublime Bach cello suites
the magic of Mona Lisa

Beauty

Frost reading *The Road Not Taken*
the healthy cry of a newborn

Your eyes, my love, your lips, your hands,
your curves, your thighs, your whole being…

The Fire

The fire under the stars
strokes your face
softly with shadows
from flickering fingers

A Caravaggio

But you glow from within
with happiness and love

A beacon to us all

When I Die

When I die, who will grieve for me,
who will shed tears when the bell tolls?

When I am no longer conscious,
no longer feeling and loving,
will you, dear, kiss me one last time,
hold my ice cold hand to your heart?

And when my body burns to ashes
or decays, devoured by maggots,
how long, love, before you forget
my face, my voice, my touch, my laugh?

When you walk through the fall forest,
swim in our pond below the falls,
will you remember our delight,
sharing such sunny summer days?

And when you lie alone at night
or naked in another's arms,
will you still evoke our great love,
the ecstasy of our coupling?

When I Die

When our children come from afar,
over dinner and lots of wine,
will you smile as you reminisce
about my quirks, faults and foibles?

When you play with our grandchildren,
sing them a song, kiss them good night,
will you gently remind them, dear,
that I loved them with all my heart?

And as you read these my poems,
my *Cello's Tears*, *sotto voce*,
will you try hard to remember
the joy of our life together?

For there will be no more of me,
only what is left in your heart.

Note: *Cello's Tears* is my first collection of poetry, published in 2015 by P.R.A. Publishing.

Haiku: Dawn's Foggy *Frisson*

dawn's foggy *frisson*
invades the space of our love:
I hold you closer

There Is No Second Chance...

There is no second chance:
from birth till our last breath
every atom of time
becomes part of the next

We can never go back
and take that stride again—
each baby step we take
leads us toward an end
where consciousness withers
and we burn, we decay

We can never go back:
there is no second chance.

About the Author

Born in Budapest, Geza Tatrallyay escaped with his family from Communist Hungary in 1956 during the Revolution, immigrating to Canada. After attending the University of Toronto Schools and serving as School Captain in his last year, he graduated with a B.A. in Human Ecology from Harvard College in 1972, and, as a Rhodes Scholar from Ontario, obtained a B.A./M.A. in Human Sciences from Oxford University in 1974. He completed his studies with a M.Sc. from London School of Economics and Politics in 1975. Geza worked as a host in the Ontario Pavilion at Expo 70 in Osaka, Japan, and represented Canada in epée fencing at the Montreal Olympics in 1976. His professional experience has included stints in government, international finance and environmental entrepreneurship. Geza is a citizen of Canada and Hungary, and as a green card holder, currently divides his time between Barnard, Vermont and San Francisco. He is married to Marcia, and their daughter, Alexandra, lives in San Francisco with husband David, and two sons, Sebastian, and Orlando, while their son, Nicholas, lives in Nairobi with his Hungarian wife, Fanni, and his granddaughter, Sophia, to whom this collection is dedicated. Geza is also the author of five novels, three memoirs, two other poetry collections from P.R.A. Publishing and a children's book.

About Peter Fox Smith

A Vermont native, Mr. Smith was raised in an artistic family with New England and mid-western roots. His love for and involvement with music, painting and poetry began naturally before he could remember and still remains. Educated at University Preparatory School, Dennison University (B.A.) and Harvard University (A.M., PhD.) he served as professor of Philosophy and dean at Emerson College (Boston), Royalton College (Vermont) and Canaan College (NH). He also taught at Dartmouth and Harvard. His love of opera he shared every Saturday on Vermont Public Radio for forty years in a program he wrote, narrated and produced. He was 13 when he began to write poetry and has never stopped. Now retired from both radio and teaching, he works exclusively on all aspects of poetry full-time; reading, writing, publishing and giving readings. Poetry, music and family are his life.

Other titles by Geza Tatrallyay from P.R.A. Publishing

Cello's Tears
ISBN:978-1-941416-08-2
Published 2015

Sighs and Murmurs
ISBN: 978-1-941416-12-9
Published 2018

For more information on Geza Tatrallyay visit http://www.gezatatrallyay.com
For more on P.R.A. Publishing visit http://www.prapublishing.com
Follow us on: Facebook Twitter Instagram

www.ingramcontent.com/pod-product-compliance
Lightning Source LLC
Chambersburg PA
CBHW030123100526
44591CB00009B/506